Original title:
The Fiddle-Leaf's Solitude

Copyright © 2025 Creative Arts Management OÜ
All rights reserved.

Author: Micah Sterling
ISBN HARDBACK: 978-1-80581-925-7
ISBN PAPERBACK: 978-1-80581-452-8
ISBN EBOOK: 978-1-80581-925-7

A Quiet Reverie Amongst the Greens

In a pot so small, it feels rather grand,
Swaying gently as I take a stand.
The dust bunnies dance, a leafy ballet,
Who knew houseplants could party this way?

Sunbeams tickle, they come and they go,
A sunny embrace, or so it would show.
I whisper my secrets, the soil my friend,
In this quiet concert, I'll never pretend.

The Longing of an Urban Plant

Windows wide open, my dreams take flight,
Watching the pigeons, such a daring sight.
Do they know I exist, with roots in the ground?
Or does my green presence just blend with the sound?

The traffic hums on the busy main street,
Can I join in too, with my leafy heartbeat?
Oh, to wander beyond this ceramic cage,
Where the world's bustling and I'm stuck with the sage.

Shadows in a Leafy Universe

A universe caught in my leaf's green embrace,
    Shadows perform on this botanical space.
The cat thinks it's hunting, so stealthy and sly,
But here in my kingdom, a leaf's the best spy!

   Tiny bugs march across my grand stage,
     Do they pirouette, or just act their age?
   In my leafy domain, I reign like a queen,
A plant with aspirations, just keeping it green.

Secrets of the Enclosed Room

In this cozy room, I stretch and I sigh,
Admiring the dust motes that dance with a pried.
The curtain whispers gossip from days long gone,
While I am the sentinel, quietly drawn.

The clock ticks away, ticking tales in the dark,
A secret confederate in this leafy park.
Who knew that my roots had such stories to tell?
In the silence of solitude, all is quite well.

Seasons of Isolation

In a pot, with no view,
Just me and my little crew.
A cactus cracked a joke one day,
But I just stood there, passively sway.

Raindrops laugh, they fall and slide,
While I sit here, arms open wide.
The sun peeks in, gives me a wink,
And off I go, deep in thought, I sink.

Winter chill, no blanket here,
Yet warm enough to hold back cheer.
A squirrel outside does a jig,
I never thought, I'd feel so big.

Ah, the seasons come and go,
While I pretend to put on a show.
The world is loud, a raucous fuss,
Yet in my pot, it's all a plus.

In the Company of Silence

Oh, the joy of quiet days,
Where drip, drop, drips count their ways.
A snail just said, 'What's with the gloom?'
I shrugged it off, this is my room.

Beetle tap dances on my stem,
I roll my eyes, up to my hem.
Lizards peek and steal a glance,
Yet here I sway, in my own trance.

When night falls, stars have a chat,
While I stand still, like a welcome mat.
The moon shares tales of days gone by,
And I nod along, oh so spry.

A breeze comes in, gives me a tease,
Swirling leaves, oh what a wheeze!
Though I'm rooted, I remain spry,
A plant with humor, who never says die.

A Leaf's Cradle of Solitude

In a corner, I think and ponder,
Surrounded by space, makes me wander.
Two leaves whisper about lost friends,
I chuckle; my solitude never ends.

A shadow dances, talks to the floor,
I giggle softly, what's behind that door?
Even dust bunnies give me a grin,
This life of mine's where fun begins.

The sun's a clown with its golden rays,
Shining bright in my leafy maze.
And every time the wind starts to play,
I laugh out loud, come what may!

Isolation teaches me all the tricks,
Like how to chuckle without fix.
Though alone, I'm never grey,
I dance in silence, come what may.

Conversations with an Empty Space

In a pot so wide and bare,
I chat with dust without a care.
My leafy friend's not here today,
I guess my jokes are just too cliché.

The sunlight spills a playful glare,
As I pretend he's sitting there.
A lint ball rolls; I laugh and sigh,
Oh, what a lonely, leafy guy!

I talk of twirls and dance of light,
The plant's a ghost; it's quite a sight.
Should I hang a sign of 'Plants Not Allowed'?
Or wait for company, shrouded in cloud?

But silence echoes back to me,
This one-sided chat is rather free.
I tell my tales to walls and air,
For now, it's just me and my bare chair.

An Oath to the Solitary Green

I pledge my heart to leafy grace,
To one great friend in an empty space.
With whispers soft and tender light,
I promise to make this lonely sight.

"No need for friends," I firmly say,
As shadows dance throughout the day.
With each new leaf, I have a cheer,
Though I admit, it feels quite queer.

A cactus rolled its eyes one night,
'You've lost your game; it's simply trite.'
But I just chuckled, tossed my hair,
My leafy pal, you're beyond compare!

In solitude, I find the fun,
With whispered tales till day is done.
An oath was made to greenery,
In laughter's arms, we'll always be.

Stylus of Succulents and Shadows

With shadows creeping on the floor,
I scribble tales, my favorite chore.
Succulents nod as if they know,
Their silent pact; it starts to grow.

I see a leaf that winks at me,
In this small space, a comedy.
A twist of fate, or just bad luck,
These stories bloom where plants are stuck.

"I'll draw you tall," I start to write,
"A masterpiece in morning light."
The pot replies with silent cheer,
A greenish grin from ear to ear.

With comic plots, we weave and spin,
Creating laughter underneath our skin.
An artist's heart, a writer's dream,
In leafy realms, we make a team.

Through Glass, Bound by Nature

Through glassy panes, I see the sun,
 Yet here I sit, oh what a pun!
My green companion cannot speak,
 In silent grace, we both feel weak.

Sunlight glimmers on dust bunnies,
A fleeting audience, no real funnies.
I tell my tales to potted friends,
Searching for laughs, but met with blends.

The leaves pretend to nod and sway,
 Yet can't discern what I convey.
"Did you hear that one?" I burst with glee,
 Only crickets in return decree.

A dance of light, a rueful glance,
In these green walls, we take our chance.
Amused by nature's quiet chime,
Two souls entwined by laughter's rhyme.

A Leaf's Diary of Dreams

In the pot, I'm a lone star,
But oh, my thoughts wander far.
Imagining parties with squirrels,
And dances with fluttering pearls.

The sun casts shadows, a silly game,
Each day I wake, it's never the same.
I gossip with raindrops, they spill the tea,
About a snail who thinks he's a marquee.

When the wind whispers a secret tune,
I giggle and sway, not a moment too soon,
My roots send signals to nearby greens,
As I concoct my leaves' wacky routines.

I pen these thoughts in my bark-bound book,
While curious bugs take a humble look.
In this houseplant life, what could be better?
Dreaming of laughter, I'll send them a letter.

Stillness in the Canopy

Up high, the world is quite a show,
But stillness does have its own glow.
The dust motes dance, with such flair,
While I sip sunlight, without a care.

The potted kingdom is calm and neat,
A throne made of soil, my leafy seat.
With no noisy neighbors, just a breeze,
I chuckle softly, can this really please?

When a breeze tickles my verdant skin,
I laugh aloud, "Let the games begin!"
A rustle here, a flutter there,
My giggles echo through the still air.

Every now and then, a bird might peek,
I wave with charm, and play hide and seek.
In this quiet space, where humor resides,
I know in stillness, my fun abides.

The Unseen Conversations of Foliage

Gathered leaves share tales untold,
In whispers soft, their secrets unfold.
A conversation of roots deep below,
Who knew that such gossip could flow?

The tiny ants march to a funky beat,
While I roll my eyes at their busy feet.
They've no time to chat, just work, work, work,
Yet somehow, they're the quirkiest perk.

A shadow darts; is that a butterfly?
Oh, please stop by and join the high fry.
We'll plan an outing to nearby blooms,
While giggles echo through earthen rooms.

In this emerald world, we're a merry crew,
With laughter and whispers, just me and you.
A leafy life, full of jests and cheer,
We bloom with joy, from far and near.

Reflections of Solitary Splendor

In sunlight pools, I dream awake,
Contemplating the right brunch to make.
I imagine a feast with cocoa and cheer,
With crumpets served up, oh, what a year!

A fleeting glance from a passing bird,
As I snicker softly, saying, "How absurd!"
Is she jealous of my stillness divine?
Or just pondering how to cross the line?

With every rustle, I conjure a jest,
Pretending my life is one grand fest.
Who knew a plant could be so spry?
In my verdant corner, I twinkle and fly.

So, here in my pot, I dance on my own,
With petals like banners, I've joyfully grown.
Reflections of mirth in greenery's hold,
This solitary splendor is worth more than gold.

Solitude Cradled in Green

In a corner sits a plant,
Dust gathers, it can't chant.
No one hears its leafy sighs,
As it dreams of sunny skies.

Wednesdays felt like forever,
Staring blankly, oh so clever.
A spider swings on a web,
Debates if it should ebb.

The pot is its only friend,
They giggle, gossip without end.
A gnome winks, gets it all wrong,
Sings off-key a silly song.

Once a cat brushed by with glee,
Now it's just the leaves and me.
Green dreams of a partner dance,
While a plant stands, lost in trance.

Echoes in the Stillness

A singleton in the corner stands,
With no marching band or fans.
Leaves whisper secrets and drink air,
In a world that doesn't care.

Oh, the joys of being green,
Waiting for the quirky scene.
Musty corners, spider's creep,
Silent watches while they sleep.

With each breeze, a quick embrace,
But no one stops to see its face.
A vacant stage, no audience near,
Leaves sing out, but no one hears.

Oh, the laughter of the dust,
In this waiting room, they trust.
One day they'll dance, it's clear,
Until then, it whispers here.

Harmonies of the Quiet Leaf

In a window, a green delight,
Strumming tunes with all its might.
Leaves rustle, a secret tune,
Inviting in the cheeky moon.

Whispers trapped in sunlight's beams,
Feeling lost in wistful dreams.
The cat jumps by, thinks it's grand,
But the plant retains its stand.

Bugs buzz by, a lively crew,
While the leaf just plays it cool.
Sighs of struggle, laughter rare,
The neither here nor there affair.

Still, it hums a lonely song,
Pretends the world is bustling along.
Harmonies float on gentle air,
In a party without a care.

Conflicts of a Leaf in Stillness

Trapped in green, what fate to choose?
Chasing sunbeams I might lose.
Leaves bicker on which way to lean,
While a shadow plays it mean.

A rubber plant mocks with flair,
As I gaze at the empty air.
Pursuing dreams of vibrant hue,
But stuck with a view that's so askew.

Who knew solitude could be fun?
Strange games played with a sunbeam run.
I'll twirl in my pot like a pro,
While pondering where all the rest go.

Imagined friends in the mist,
All enjoying life I've missed.
A leaf's plight in peace refined,
Yet in quiet, chuckles you might find.

Embracing the Lonesome Green

In a pot, I stand alone,
With roots that look for friends,
A cactus waves from next door,
But spines, they make amends.

Sunshine dances on my leaves,
While dust bunnies take their strolls,
Chatting with the swinging chair,
And laughing at the moles.

A spider's web is quite the catch,
From leaves to shelf, it's strung so fine,
I call him Fred, a loyal mate,
He's busy weaving my punchline.

So here I sway, with all my grace,
A lonesome plant, but not forlorn,
With every rustle, I'm a star,
In my green world, I am reborn.

Living in Leafy Solitude

In my leafy fort, I reside,
No need for chats or coffee times,
The gentle breeze becomes my guide,
Nature's whispers, silly rhymes.

A fellow fern peeks over sly,
We trade our jokes beneath the light,
While gnats perform a dance nearby,
I chuckle at their awkward flight.

Conversations with the sunlight,
And shadows play their fleeting game,
A small bouquet of blooms in sight,
Each wave of green, they know my name.

The empty room? A cozy space,
Where laughter blooms, though I'm alone,
In solitude, I've found my place,
In leafy laughs, I've really grown.

Eclipsed by Nature's Walls

Walls of green, they hug me tight,
As if to cage my leafy glee,
But oh, the joy of day and night,
Where shadows play and dance with me.

I share a laugh with leaf and vine,
In this quiet, leafy sprawl,
While ants parade like heroes fine,
Their tiny war feels big and tall.

A light breeze tickles my broad leaves,
I giggle like a child at play,
Together, we form secret weaves,
While nature's giggles sweep the day.

In my little world, I'm the queen,
No noise but rustles, soft and small,
And amidst the greens, I'm rarely seen,
Eclipsed by nature's joyful thrall.

Worthy Companions of Silence

In silence, I find humor grand,
No need for chatter, just a grin,
The quiet speaks, with leafy band,
Together, we enjoy the win.

A single droplet bright as day,
Rolls down a leaf, a race it starts,
While neighboring plants cheer away,
We giggle softly; life imparts.

The lonely tick of time's sweet clock,
Each second drips like morning dew,
In my solitude, I'll rock,
With leafy friends who stick like glue.

So here I stand, the green recluse,
In laughter born from silence found,
Worthy companions, no excuse,
In solitude, my joy abounds.

Resting in Verdant Silence

In a corner, much to tease,
A lonely leaf sways with ease.
The sunlight laughs, the shadow grins,
Whispers of nature, where it begins.

With every breeze, a gentle sway,
It dreams of friends that went away.
A pot of dirt, its only mate,
Yet still it dances, a leafy fate.

In solitude, it finds a tune,
A melody of leaf and moon.
Pretending not to feel its fate,
While crickets join to celebrate!

Oh, what a sight, this leafy glee,
A leaf who thinks it's wild and free.
While still it sits, in quiet poise,
The world outside, a sea of noise.

The Unsung Leaf's Tale

Once a leaf sought fame and glory,
It longed to be the star of the story.
But in its pot, it plots alone,
While plants around it groan and moan.

With soilmates not quite up to par,
It dreams of being a shining star.
A leaf with flair, a knack for heights,
Yet here it clings through silent nights.

Each dust mote that floats feels like praise,
In the quiet, it weaves its ways.
Conversations with shadows, quite absurd,
With daisies thinking it's quite unheard.

So here it sits, in unaware bliss,
Missing the chance for that leafy kiss.
The world keeps spinning, but that's just fine,
For a leaf alone can still shine divine.

An Ode to the Isolated Leaf

To a leaf that stands quite still,
Adventures sought, yet none to fill.
With laughter from the breezy air,
It dreams of tales beyond compare.

While others shake in joyful play,
Our leaf just nods, then looks away.
A quirky leaf, with humor vast,
In every sigh, a jolly cast.

It waves to spiders, gives them spunk,
And speaks to shadows, never shrunk.
A poet's heart in a plant's embrace,
Finding joy in the smallest space.

So cheers to leaves that hold a jest,
In solitude, they truly are blessed.
With each green blade a story sown,
In quiet corners, humor's grown.

Solitude Draped in Green

A lone leaf in a bustling room,
Where laughter echoes, giving gloom.
Yet here it thrives, without a care,
Telling jokes to the autumn air.

Each day it stretches, with leafy flair,
Imagining the tales it might share.
With silly winds that dance about,
It creates laughs no one's about.

Sipping sunlight like a mug of tea,
Pondering why it's still so free.
A method to its leafy groove,
In solitude, it finds its move.

So let it be, the leaf who sings,
Laughing at life's comical things.
In a world so vast, it's clear to see,
Solitude sometimes feels like glee.

A Solitary Whisper

In a corner, leafy green,
Stands a plant, quite unseen.
It awaits a friendly chatter,
But all it hears is silence's patter.

With a twist, it seeks a joke,
But the laughter's just a yoke.
The wall's the only one to hear,
Its puns fall flat, that's quite clear.

A sunbeam sneaks, a touch of light,
Yet still it feels alone at night.
It dreams of friends, a leafy crew,
But parties are just a notion or two.

Oh, to dance with others' grace,
Instead, it sways in empty space.
Yet in its heart, a giggle grows,
For it knows, some goofiness shows.

Dreaming in the Shadows

In the shade of a cozy nook,
A plant dreams of a funny book.
Its leaves, they rustle with delight,
Imagining jokes in the pale moonlight.

A passing bug makes it laugh out loud,
Yet, it's still there, alone and proud.
The shadows giggle with each breeze,
As it plots to tickle the tall trees.

One leaf sighs, 'Why so shy?'
Another whispers, 'Let's give it a try!'
They dance beneath the stars so bright,
In the dreams, they are quite the sight.

Yet morning comes, their dreams all fade,
Sunbeams break the night-time shade.
Still, the plant knows, with a wink or two,
That laughter in the dark feels true.

The Leaf's Unshared Sunlight

Alone it basks in the bright warm sun,
Yet it longs for a friend for some fun.
The rays dance down, a lively jest,
But without laughter, it feels suppressed.

"Oh, pour some joy upon my leaves,
Bring along the giggles and the heaves!"
But sunlight's just a glowing tease,
As it sways gently, yearning to please.

Daydreams of chats with roses and buds,
Instead, it charts the rain's soft floods.
With humor stitched in every vein,
Its solitude sways like a soft refrain.

Still it chuckles at the bees at play,
With their buzzing banter every day.
And whispers to those passing by,
"Join my leaves, let's reach for the sky!"

Threads of Solitude in the Breeze

In the breeze, a whisper glows,
Woven threads of lonely prose.
Nobody sees its gentle sway,
As it daydreams the hours away.

A breeze strolls in, sets a prank,
Leaves quaking, a giggling bank.
"I could use a friend," it sighs,
"Someone to share these silly tries."

It spins tales of mischief divine,
While shadows laugh at the punchline.
But still, it stands with leaves outstretched,
Waiting for jokes, a feeling fetched.

Yet the wind just blows and jesters tease,
With rustling tunes, it sways with ease.
For even alone, in nature's song,
It finds the humor, where it belongs.

Dreams of a Windowed Wanderer

In the sunbeam I perk and lean,
A leafy throne, yet feel unseen.
I dream of jungles wild and vast,
While plotting how to escape at last.

A small breeze tickles my grand leaf,
I giggle softly in disbelief.
Nature's wonders call my name,
But old pot life is rather tame.

I sway and shiver with delight,
Imagining a daring flight.
But down I stay, a potted star,
My dreams of travel always far.

Oh to roam where wild things play,
Instead, I dance in this display.
With each twist, I scheme and plan,
For a windowed wanderer's grand new span.

Nestled in Nature's Embrace

Here I sit, a plant so spry,
In a corner, pondering why.
A sunbeam warms my glossy skin,
While dust bunnies laugh in their kin.

The cats wander by with curious glares,
As I flinch, pretending no cares.
Oh, to prance in fields so wide,
But here I stand, with pride, I hide.

An indoor life can be absurd,
Especially with that chirping bird.
Each day I'm trapped in this cocoon,
Imagining adventures under the moon.

My toes are roots, yet heart will soar,
Wishing for an open door.
Still, I chuckle at my fate,
Nature's jest is worth the wait.

Retreat of the Potted Soul

I sit in silence, leafy and meek,
My pot's a fortress, or so I speak.
But within these walls, I'm quite the sage,
Plotting shenanigans, page by page.

The humans fuss, they can't quite know,
The whimsy that makes my spirit glow.
As I scheme for a wondrous fling,
I realize how silly it all can sing.

Each raindrop that falls makes me giggle,
Flashes of sunshine make me wiggle.
But oh, my roots keep me confined,
To this pot-life, eternally entwined.

Down here, I'm a silly fool,
Planning jumps into the cool.
With every thought, I feel quite spry,
Retreating smartly, I ponder why.

The Silent Chorus of Indoor Flora

Whispers among the leafy throng,
A quiet chant, yet feels so wrong.
Potted pals, we roll our eyes,
At the humans' busy, petty lies.

Each morning, we stretch in light,
Gossip of bugs that took off in flight.
"We could rule the room," said a fern,
"If only we could just discern!"

A cactus grins with prickly pride,
While succulents suppress their wild side.
In our green retreat, we laugh and plot,
Secret meetings in the flowerpot.

The world outside is vast and grand,
Yet here we laugh at life's command.
With every stem and leaf, we sing,
In the irony of indoor bling.

Solitary Canopy

Up high, I dance with the breeze,
While down low, dust bunnies tease.
Birds chatter, but I'm all alone,
A leafy queen on a leafy throne.

Sunlight flickers, a playful prank,
I wave my leaves, give a little flank.
A smile from roots, totally absurd,
Living my life with the silliest bird.

Droplets gather, dear rain, do stay,
I'm making a hat for my birthday play.
Wind whispers jokes that I can't quite catch,
But laughing with clouds, I just can't match.

Yet here I stand, my green, proud show,
Nature's awkward but charming flow.
A lonely titan in a garden grand,
With roots that hold the world in hand.

Confessions of a Leafy Enigma

I ponder deep in my leafy head,
Why do squirrels treat me like their bed?
Under my shade, they will convene,
Making my branches their morning scene.

A curious fate, this leafy plight,
To offer a shade for their little bite.
They nibble and chatter, totally absurd,
I'll write a book: 'My Life with a Bird.'

Whispers of wind are my only friends,
While my leafy laughter never ends.
I twirl around, a leafy ballet,
Holding my secrets till the break of day.

I guard my thoughts, so leafy divine,
In my little patch, I sip sunshine.
For every joke that in me hides,
I carry the laughter that nature abides.

The Quiet Embrace of Nature

In silence, I stretch toward the blue,
Feeling the thrill of a breeze that's new.
Curled up tight, my leaves go shy,
Wondering silently, "Am I a pie?"

Here comes a butterfly, dressed to impress,
Whispering secrets, looking quite fresh.
I try to giggle, but stifle a sneeze,
Could this be nature's form of tease?

Each drip of dew is a ticklish tease,
While ants below scurry with evident ease.
A tick on my trunk, who shall I blame?
Giggling softly, I ponder their name.

Yet with a rustle, I sway with glee,
Nature's humor is the best to be.
In this cozy world, I strive to belong,
With leaves that dance like a silly song.

Shadows Beneath the Canopy

Here in my shade, the world feels still,
A party for shadows, a whimsical thrill.
Frogs croak softly, a rhythm so strange,
  While I oversee this leafy exchange.

Laughter of leaves has a sound so sweet,
As critters skip around, oh what a feat!
I play the hostess, feeling quite proud,
  In my leafy hair, a dewdrop crowd.

Celestial scenes through tree branches peek,
  Ushering dreams, though I barely speak.
Nature whispers jokes, it's an inside game,
While I chuckle softly in sunshine's name.

Caterpillars wiggle in their comical plight,
Chasing their dreams in the soft moonlight.
With a giggle and sway, I'll hold them near,
For even in solitude, there's much to cheer.

The Lonesome Path Among Greenery

Amidst the trees, I wander slow,
Chasing squirrels, putting on a show.
Leaves rustle like they laugh and tease,
I trip on roots, oh, what a breeze!

A plant in shade, just hangs around,
Whispers secrets without a sound.
Nature grins, it finds me funny,
Under the sun, it feels so punny!

Friends with worms that crawl and squirm,
I tell them jokes, they love the term.
A lonesome path, yet not a bore,
With every stumble, I crave for more!

So cheers to leaves in merry glee,
In this green crowd, there's room for me.
I've got my pals, though they don't speak,
In solitude, we thrive, not weak!

A Leaf's Solace in Stillness

A single leaf rests, struck with glee,
Staying silent like it's sipping tea.
It stretches wide, with arms so bold,
"Come join," it smiles, "let's not grow old!"

Oh, bumblebees buzz by and chat,
While I stand still, that's where it's at!
In stillness found, I softly chuckle,
Eavesdropping on nature's little struggle.

The sun shines bright, my shadow's tall,
Yet here I sit, without a call.
"Hey, Mr. Pine, don't be so shy!
Watch me dance, let's give it a try!"

Roots below play tricks on me,
As I sway, carefree, oh so free!
Laughter echoes in the breeze,
A solo show among the trees!

Muted Harmonies of Solitude

In the quiet space where shadows play,
Giggles hide in the grass all day.
Whispers bounce through branches high,
While clouds just hover, passing by.

Oh, the stillness carries a jest,
As flowers bloom, they feel so blessed.
But a silly gnome steals all the shine,
With a rusty fork and an old red vine!

Crickets chirp; they sing along,
Dancing lightly, they find their song.
The sun beams down, a playful light,
In muted tones, we dance at night.

So while alone, I find my groove,
Nature's rhythm, it helps me move.
In solitude, I notice my power,
Beneath the leaves, I bloom like a flower!

A Quiet Heart Amongst the Leaves

Amidst the foliage, I pause and think,
My heart is quiet, yet I just wink.
With each soft rustle, a giggle slips,
Through leafy curtains, nature tips!

A snail on a mission, oh so slow,
Comes for a chat and shares a joke.
"Why so glum?" I pull my face,
"Join the fun, let's pick up the pace!"

The branches sway, in jest they sway,
While shadows dance, come out and play!
A quiet heart, but laughter rings,
In this leafy realm, joy brightly springs.

So here I linger, feeling the thrill,
Amongst the leaves, I've found my fill.
In solitude, we make quite the pair,
With giggles and grins to share everywhere!

Beneath the Veil of the Canopy

A leaf hangs low, it wants to dance,
But the squirrels laugh, in a wild prance.
"Come join!" they shout, with their furry flair,
Yet all the leaf does is sway in despair.

A breeze flirts by, teasing the stem,
"You look quite lonely, my leafy friend!"
"I have no partners for a leafy jig,
Just me and my thoughts—ouch, that's the twig!"

Sunlight flickers, like a light chat,
While shadows gossip beneath the mat.
The leaf pretends, with a flick and a toss,
As if it cares, though it feels quite the loss.

So beneath the green, in awkward cheer,
The laughter echoes for all to hear.
Yet in its heart, the leaf pretends,
To be as vibrant as all its friends.

The Whispers of Branches Above

The branches gossip, with no one to see,
Telling tales of the leaf, under the tree.
"Oh, did you hear? It tried to sway!"
"No one to dance with, just lonely play."

The shadows chuckle, casting their shade,
Over the leaf that wishes it stayed.
"Why test the breeze? You're set for a fall!"
"It's better than sitting, alone at the hall!"

There's humor in lofty, tall branches tall,
As they sway and wave while leaf does stall.
"Join us!" they beckon, with playful glee,
"Stop sulking there, under our canopy!"

Yet as they tease, the leaf holds its ground,
In this merry jest, solitude is found.
For in each flutter, a giggle is born,
Amid quiet laughter, it dreams of the dawn.

Green Silhouettes of the Alone

In hues of green, a shadow does creep,
Where sunlight drips, like a secret peep.
Silhouettes twist, as if each one knows,
The leaf, aptly named, shows off its woes.

It tries to stand tall, with graceful flair,
While bugs fly past, without a care.
"Watch out, you twig!" they giggle and soar,
As the leaf just quivers, hoping for more.

Beneath the cheer of a laughing tree,
The leaf contemplates, could it ever be free?
"Just one little jig, one leap in the air!"
Yet no one is listening, for all just stares.

In silhouettes, it dreams up a dance,
To twirl and flutter, would be the chance.
But stuck in its stillness, it sighs with a moan,
While shadows pretend they are never alone.

Lifting the Weight of Quiet Shadows

With whispers soft, the shadows conspire,
To make the leaf feel just a bit higher.
"Join us in laughter, it's a grand day!"
Yet still it ponders, where's the ballet?

The wind tickles gently, a sweet serenade,
While the leaf just droops, in a lazy charade.
"Up here, we're merry! Here, bold! Here, bright!"
Wants to join in, but feels freeze-frame fright.

A joke from the bark about getting too stuck,
While the leaf just sighs, "Well, that's my luck."
For every chuckle rides the cool breeze,
Yet it's flapping alone, just trying to please.

As shadows linger and giggles ignite,
The leaf stands in silence, waiting for light.
So lifting the weight, a droll tale unfolds,
Of solitude's dance, and the laugh it upholds.

Whispers of the Verdant Heart

In a corner pot, a leaf took a seat,
Dreaming of trips and tasty sunbeams sweet.
It shook in the breeze, feeling quite tall,
While dust bunnies giggled, watching it sprawl.

A squirrel passed by, with a donut in paw,
The leaf called out loud, "Hey, can I have a jaw?"
But the squirrel just winked, and scampered away,
Leaving the leaf with its thoughts on display.

It practiced its dance, like a star on a stage,
But only the shadows would turn the next page.
With a chuckle or two, it spun 'round with glee,
While snoring houseplants rolled their eyes at the spree.

So it swayed and it twisted, with laughter so spry,
Wishing for friends who could chat by and by.
And though all alone in its leafy green chair,
The flower pots whispered - "The show's beyond compare!"

The Lonesome Green Sentinel

A lone little sprout on a windowsill bare,
Tried to grow out a cape, but it just wasn't there.
It frowned at the curtains and sighed with a huff,
"Isn't being green supposed to be fun enough?"

With a sly little wink, it practiced a pose,
While rubber bands giggled, hanging round its toes.
"Watch me become a tree!" it declared to a shoe,
But the shoe just said, "That's not what I'd do."

A curious snail with a shell made of bling,
Slid up to the sprout, said, "Hey, that's the thing!
Grow tall and wear shades, get the party up high,
We'll dance under raindrops, just you and I!"

The sprout then stood proud, with its newfound bold friend,
Moving and grooving, no sign of an end.
Together they laughed with whimsical glee,
In a world full of wonders, just them, wild and free!

Thoughts Among the Treetops

Once there was a leaf, perched high and quite grand,
Daydreaming adventures, plotting a band.
"Who's up for a jam?" it loudly proclaimed,
But the air just chuckled, leaving it shamed.

With an acorn on drums and a twig on guitar,
It practiced for hours beneath a bright star.
The wind would hum softly, adding a tune,
While the clouds drifted by, like a waiting balloon.

When night came a-knocking, the sprout got all shy,
"Is it silly to hope for a friend in the sky?"
But the stars winked down, with their twinkling delight,
Saying, "Join us in dancing, you're here in the night!"

So the leaf shuffled joyfully, swaying with glee,
Under a shroud of giggles, just it and the spree.
While the world lay sleeping, the leaf found its beat,
In dreams among treetops, where the funny ones meet.

Resolute in Quietude

Nestled in dust, a plant took a stand,
Watching the world, a quirky demand.
"It's hard being green and just sitting so still,
While the dust particles ride like a phantom thrill!"

Yet, in the stillness, it found quite a laugh,
From the jokes of the soil and a worm's clear gaffe.
"Hey, you there, chub!" the pot called with flair,
"Join us for tea! We won't go anywhere!"

With a chuckle and cover, they huddled so tight,
The leaf told some stories of great leafy might.
Around the small room, laughter rang like a bell,
As friends gathered 'round, under the plant's cozy shell.

Though still quite alone in its corner so sweet,
It thrived on the humor of friends that it'd meet.
In the heart of the green, with a grin so unbound,
The quiet little world created its sound.

Solitary in a Sea of Sunlight

In a pot, I sway and dance,
With leaves like sails, in a sunlit trance.
The world's a buzz, but here I'm still,
Watching shadows play, oh what a thrill!

I overhear whispers of garden chats,
While I sip sunlight, donned in my flats.
The daisies gossip, their petals aflutter,
I chuckle softly, and spill some butter!

Breezes tickle, I tickle back,
I'm king of this green, on my leafy track.
Yet when the raindrops rise to sing,
I'm just a splash, a wobbly thing!

Oh, the world may think I'm quite aloof,
But inside this pot, I'm the goofball proof!
So call me sprout with a sunny side,
In this sunny sea, I'll take my pride!

Through the Stillness, a Story Blooms

A quiet leaf, like a comical seam,
Waiting for dramas, a soap opera dream.
The sunlight dribbles, the shadows play,
And bugs reenact my favorite ballet!

I watch as the ants, in suits so neat,
Plot their next snack, a picnic treat.
With popcorn leaves, and frond-shaped cakes,
Their tiny parade is what nature makes!

The squirrels pass by, with acorn flair,
I giggle from branches, 'Do pull up a chair!'
For party time's when laughter's found,
In this stillness, joy knows no bounds.

Each rustle whispers a tale once told,
Of daring deeds and legends bold.
In my green safe haven, where stories loom,
A hearty chuckle waits to bloom!

Reflections in a Glass Garden

In a bowl of glass, I sit and gleam,
A leafy figure, living the dream.
Reflections dance like playful sprites,
In every glimmer, joy ignites!

I peer at the window, what do I see?
A family picnicking, laughter and glee.
Tiny hands toss crumbs, a feast for all,
While I munch on sunlight, feeling tall!

Yet, here I stay, in my careful zone,
On display like art, but still alone.
I wave to the gardener, they wave back too,
Enchanting camaraderie, just me and the dew!

Through leaf and light, reflections glint,
Of all the silly antics that nature hints.
In this glassy haven, I find my cheer,
Where laughter's the melody, bright and clear!

Heartbeats Beneath the Canopy

Beneath green splendor, I catch a sigh,
Heartbeats of foliage, oh my, oh my!
I wiggle my leaves with quite the flair,
As squirrels above start their wild affair.

They scamper and chatter, a raucous crew,
While I just giggle from my leafy view.
The slugs slowly slide, with a charming grace,
I cheer them on, in this leafy race!

The butterflies flutter, a colorful spree,
Dancing and laughing right next to me.
I join the ballet, on my dear branch,
With twirls and sways, I take a chance!

Oh, underneath this cheerful dome,
Where giggles bounce and vegetables roam.
My heart beats loud, in the sunlit air,
Amongst all this joy, I'm always aware!

The Loneliness of a Leafy Companion

In a corner, green and shy,
A leafy friend lets out a sigh.
With all the dust and silent strife,
It dreams of dances, a leaf's wild life.

Each day it waits for a breeze to come,
To lift its spirits, oh so glum.
But only cats stroll by and tease,
Leaving it lonely with just the sneeze.

A curious spider weaves its thread,
In the shade where the leaf there bled.
They share the silent laughs and woes,
A duo that nobody knows.

The plant might ponder, "Where's my crew?"
With a grin as wide as morning dew.
But every day is a new routine,
Just waiting for fun that's never seen.

Nature's Silent Witness

A shrub with secrets, bold and grand,
Stands quiet, like a statue planned.
It peers at squirrels with a watchful eye,
As they chase their tails and jump up high.

Whispers of tales in the rustling leaves,
Of garden parties it never believes.
"Shall I dance?" it dreams with glee,
But all it gets is honeybees' decree.

The flowers laugh, they twirl and sway,
While our silent friend just sits in dismay.
It thinks of jokes they wouldn't dare share,
But no one listens, no one's aware.

Oh, the burden of watching nature's game,
A quiet witness, it feels so lame.
Yet still, it chuckles at the birds' free tune,
Wishing for friends by the light of the moon.

Secrets in the Shade

In the shady nook, where sunlight weeps,
A leafy host, while the world just sleeps.
It craves laughter like it craves the rain,
Yet stands alone, feeling quite insane.

Rustles of whispers through branches near,
But squirrels won't share their snack or cheer.
They giggle and dart, leaving it pout,
While it sighs softly, "What's this about?"

A cricket hops on to crack a joke,
But he's only a joker with no cloak.
Together they giggle at shadows they see,
While leaves rustle laughter, carefree and free.

"A party of one," it thinks with a grin,
"Inviting the world to dance in my skin."
Yet the birds just sing to the sky so wide,
While the shade-grounded fellow keeps secrets inside.

A Melody Written in Green

In the heart of the garden, odd but sly,
A leafy figure gives a wistful sigh.
It dreams of rhythms, of beats so sweet,
But all it hears is bugs on repeat.

Oh, to dance in a symphony grand,
With breezes that hum and softly command.
Yet here it sits, with a view to behold,
While petals around it burst out bold.

It sings to the toad, with a croak and a twist,
While sunlight dapples, and shadows persist.
"What's my tune?" it croons to the sky,
But only the frogs answer, with a lullaby.

And though it feels like a leaf out of place,
It sways in the quiet, with charm and grace.
For every beat that the world may know,
In green solitude, a melody will glow.

Shadowed Resilience

In the corner it stands, full of flair,
Pretending it loves the cool, crisp air.
Its broad leaves flap in the silent night,
Hoping for company, but luck's out of sight.

The dust bunnies dance, their laughter on mute,
While it braces for storms like a charming brute.
Mr. Spider stops by, a friend for a day,
Then scuttles away; it's back to dismay.

One would think that it'd join in the fun,
But every new leaf hides from the sun.
With each little breeze, a little leaf sighs,
"Why don't I bloom with a pair of green thighs?"

Yet somehow it thrives, an odd little tree,
Surrounded by socks and dust-coated debris.
With a quirky stance, it's a brown-thumb's delight,
In the heart of the home, it brings smiles at night.

Solitary Symphony in Green

Oh, leafy companion with no one to boast,
You sway to a symphony, a soloist's host.
Though the chorus is silent, your stem stays so grand,
In this room full of laughter, you'll take a stand.

With sunlight a-dancing upon your green stage,
You flick your broad leaves, feeling quite sage.
"Why don't they chat? Can't they see my great flair?"
If only the cats would just stop and stare!

The furniture hides all its plans for a dance,
While you grip to your soil in a solitary trance.
If a lively tune played, you'd shake to the beat,
But alas, it's just you and your awkward green feat.

So here's to the green with a coat of fine gloss,
May it never grow weary or measure its loss.
For who needs a crowd when you've got solid ground?
In the end, it might just be you that's profound!

Thoughts from the Quiet Verdure

Nestled in shadows, a thinker at heart,
Whispering secrets in the dim of a part.
With roots deep in wonder, it ponders the day,
"Will I ever get visitors? Please, let them stay!"

Each leaf is a letter, each stem a soft sigh,
Yearning for chatter as clouds drift on by.
A pot of green dreams all wrapped in a shell,
You'd think it was spare, yet it wishes for swell.

"Do I wear mismatched socks? Should I make a show?"
As dust bunnies gather, it sidles down low.
Just trying to mingle with life far and near,
Yet left in this stillness, its humor's sincere.

So raise a green glass for the one who awaits,
A solitary spirit with imaginative traits.
For in thoughts and a giggle, this plant sings a tune,
That whispers 'be merry' beneath the bright moon.

Dreams of a Withered Stem

Once stood so proud, with leaves that were grand,
Now just a shadow, a tip of the hand.
As the soil turns dry, does it plot a retreat?
Or laugh at its fate with a comical feat?

In dreams it envisions a forest of fun,
With parties and breezes under warmth from the sun.
But here in the corner, the curtain is drawn,
With each wilting leaf, its hopes seem forsworn.

But lo! A new sprout breaks ground in its dreams,
What if it danced with those quirky moonbeams?
Who could've foreseen such a lively embrace?
Turning gloom into giggles in green's daring chase.

So old weary stem, keep dreaming awake,
For the laughter of life, you easily make.
With a wiggle and jiggle, who knows what's in store?
You might just rediscover what joy's truly for!

Contemplating Growth in Seclusion

In the corner, green and tall,
A plant ponders, does it call?
Leaves like hands, reaching out wide,
But no one's here, it can't confide.

Sunlight beams, but it won't chat,
Basking quietly, imagine that!
When a breeze blows through the day,
It giggles softly, then sways away.

Dust bunnies form a fluffy crew,
They cheer it on, who knew, who knew?
Hypnotized by plant-hood's plight,
Ferns are gossiping, what a sight!

So here's to leaves and all their dreams,
In silent rooms, they plot and scheme.
Who knew a pot could think so grand?
Secret thoughts in a leafy land!

Longing for a Breath of Fresh Air

In a room, so snug and tight,
A green friend hopes for flight.
Twisting leaves, it ponders why,
Only shadows pass it by.

A lonely sigh beneath the light,
It dreams of branches, oh! So bright!
With funny thoughts of trees so free,
Green confessions, just it and we.

It dreams of gusts, a playful friend,
To swoosh its leaves till daylight's end.
But alas, it can't escape this place,
Just roots and soil in a pot's embrace.

So whispers float in the close air,
To no one but the chair and stair.
What a thing, to be so bold,
While trapped in concrete, dust, and mold!

The Weight of Stillness Amidst Growth

A sturdy trunk, so steadfast,
Stillness weighs, a shadow cast.
Leaves watch time with sleepy eyes,
Wondering when the world complies.

Neighbors pass with hurried fate,
Plant just waits, it's not irate.
Roots buried deep, a wise old sage,
Jokes about this golden cage.

Oh, the tales stuck in its limbs,
Of epic quests on sunlight whims!
Yet here it stands, a statue shy,
Wishing for a daring fly.

Patience, they say, is a virtue grand,
But vines want more than just to stand.
A chuckle here, a belly laugh,
In a pot, it's half a gaffe!

Solitary Stalks and Softlight

A single stalk, so proud and tall,
Wonders if it's seen at all.
Softlight dapples, a playful tease,
It whispers back, "I'm not a sneeze!"

Around it spins the idle dust,
In its own world, it learns to trust.
Cocooned in a soft, leafy bliss,
Who knew solitude could feel like this?

It practices jokes with furry friends,
Each tiny spider? There's no end!
Laughter echoes, or maybe not,
In a quiet pot, it laughs a lot.

So here it grows, with grace and flair,
Dreaming of adventures, oh, to share!
Leaves turned up in a cheeky pose,
For in stillness, the humor flows!

www.ingramcontent.com/pod-product-compliance
Lightning Source LLC
Chambersburg PA
CBHW070336120526
44590CB00017B/2912